M000251896

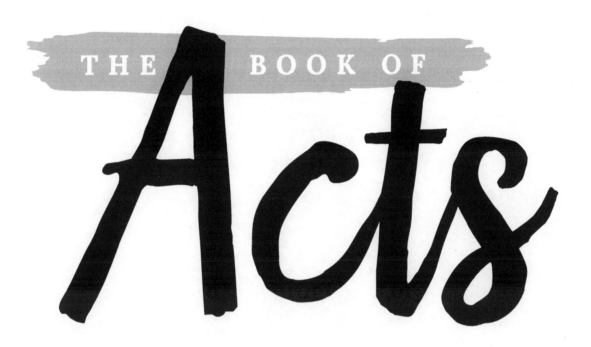

THE BOOK OF Acts

ONE CHAPTER A DAY

GoodMorningGirls.org

The Book of Acts

© 2015 Women Living Well Ministries, LLC

ALL RIGHTS RESERVED

No part of this book may be reproduced in any form or by any electronic or mechanical means, including information storage and retrieval systems, without written permission from the author, except in the case of a reviewer, who may quote brief passages embodied in critical articles or in a review.

Scripture is from the ESV® Bible (The Holy Bible, English Standard Version®), copyright © 2001 by Crossway Bibles, a publishing ministry of Good News Publishers. Used by permission. All rights reserved.

Welcome to Good Morning Girls! We are so glad you are joining us.

God created us to walk with Him, to know Him, and to be loved by Him. He is our living well, and when we drink from the water He continually provides, His living water will change the entire course of our lives.

> *Jesus said: "Whoever drinks of the water that I will give him will never be thirsty again. The water that I will give him will become in him a spring of water welling up to eternal life." ~ John 4:14 (ESV)*

So let's begin.

The method we use here at GMG is called the **SOAK** method.

- ❒ **S**—The S stands for *Scripture*—Read the chapter for the day. Then choose 1-2 verses and write them out word for word. (There is no right or wrong choice—just let the Holy Spirit guide you.)

- ❒ **O**—The O stands for *Observation*—Look at the verse or verses you wrote out. Write 1 or 2 observations. What stands out to you? What do you learn about the character of God from these verses? Is there a promise, command or teaching?

- ❒ **A**—The A stands for *Application*—Personalize the verses. What is God saying to you? How can you apply them to your life? Are there any changes you need to make or an action to take?

- ❒ **K**—The K stands for *Kneeling in Prayer*—Pause, kneel and pray. Confess any sin God has revealed to you today. Praise God for His word. Pray the passage over your own life or someone you love. Ask God to help you live out your applications.

SOAK God's word into your heart and squeeze every bit of nourishment you can out of each day's scripture reading. Soon you will find your life transformed by the renewing of your mind!

Walk with the King!

Courtney

WomenLivingWell.org, GoodMorningGirls.org

Join the GMG Community

Share your daily SOAK at 7:45am on **Facebook.com/GoodMorningGirlsWLW**

Instagram: WomenLivingWell #GoodMorningGirls

GMG Bible Coloring Chart

COLORS	KEYWORDS
PURPLE	God, Jesus, Holy Spirit, Saviour, Messiah
PINK	women of the Bible, family, marriage, parenting, friendship, relationships
RED	love, kindness, mercy, compassion, peace, grace
GREEN	faith, obedience, growth, fruit, salvation, fellowship, repentance
YELLOW	worship, prayer, praise, doctrine, angels, miracles,power of God, blessings
BLUE	wisdom, teaching, instruction, commands
ORANGE	prophecy, history, times, places, kings, genealogies, people, numbers, covenants, vows, visions, oaths, future
BROWN/GRAY	Satan, sin, death, hell, evil, idols, false teachers, hypocrisy, temptation

Introduction to the Book of Acts

The book of Acts is a unique book because it is transitional. It transitions us from the time of Christ in the Gospels to the time of the church, in the Epistles. In Acts we see, the ascension of Christ and the beginning of the great commission where the gospel leaves Jerusalem and heads to the uttermost parts of the earth—and eventually right to us today.

Purpose: Acts was written so we could see the birth and growth of the church and the acts of the Apostles.

Author: Luke (also the author of the Gospel of Luke)

Date: Estimated to be around AD 63-70

Key Verse: Acts 1:8 "But you will receive power when the Holy Spirit has come upon you, and you will be my witnesses in Jerusalem and in all Judea and Samaria, and to the end of the earth."

In the book of Acts, we start with the accession of Jesus and then head into the ministry of Peter. There, we find the establishment and expansion of the church in the first 12 chapters.

We also see Saul converted from being a persecutor of the church to a great missionary of the church. His conversion takes places in Acts 9, but we don't see his ministry really take off until chapter 13.

Themes:

There are several major themes in the book of Acts that will not only teach us about the early church but are applicable to our own lives as believers.

1. **The Holy Spirit**—Jesus promised the disciples that the Holy Spirit would come. The Holy Spirit came with power in Acts 2. He came to be our comforter, our teacher, and He is the power behind all that we do as believers. Nothing we do is by our own power but by His power that lives inside of us.

2. **The Church**—The establishment and organization of the local church is a main story line and theme of the book of Acts. The new church had many issues much like the church today. Acts gives us a lot of great examples of how to persevere in spite of problems in our church. It also talks greatly about the churches growth.

3. **Missions/Witnessing**—At the end of each gospel, Jesus left us with a commission. (Matthew 28:16-20, Mark 16:14-16, Luke 24:44-53, John 20:21-23) With this in mind, we know that this is the purpose of the church – to share the gospel! We must tell others. This expands not just the local church, but the entire Church universally. We also see in the book of Acts, that sharing the Gospel might come with a price but it strengthens our faith as we rely on God during those times.

4. **Persecution**—The church and those who defended it suffered much persecution. The same is true today. Those who stand by the doctrines and beliefs of the church might suffer opposition or persecution. The book of Acts gives encouragement to stand firm in our faith, and to remember those who have stood firm before us.

Final Thoughts:

The book of Acts is going to take us on a journey of faith. It calls Christians to live outside of their comfort zone and walk boldly to share the gospel in a world that does not seek to know God. May we be encouraged as we read the acts of those who went before us and learn that we too can persevere in an age where the Gospel is not popular.

Special Thanks

I want to extend a special thank you to Mandy Kelly, Rosilind Jukic, Bridget Childress and Misty Leask for your help with this journal. Your love, dedication and leadership to the Good Morning Girls ministry is such a blessing to all. Thank you for giving to the Lord.

~ Courtney

But you will receive power when the Holy Spirit has come upon you, and you will be my witnesses in Jerusalem and in all Judea and Samaria, and to the end of the earth."

Acts 1:8

Reflection Question:

The Apostles knew they needed to replace Judas; therefore, they trusted God to place the right person in that position.

How can we apply this principle to the relationships in our own lives?

Acts 1

S—The S stands for *Scripture*

O—The O stands for *Observation*

A—The A stands for *Application*

K—The K stands for *Kneeling in Prayer*

Everyone who calls

upon the name of the Lord

shall be saved.

Acts 2:21

Reflection Question:

Outsiders looking in thought Jesus's followers were drunk because they were so filled with the Holy Spirit.

When others look at you, can they tell you are filled with the Holy Spirit as well?

Acts 2

S—The S stands for *Scripture*

O—The O stands for *Observation*

A—The A stands for *Application*

K—The K stands for *Kneeling in Prayer*

In the name of Jesus Christ of Nazareth,

rise up and walk!

Acts 3:6

Reflection Question:

While the people were in awe over the lame man's healing, Peter took that chance to direct the people's attention to God.

In what ways can we apply this to those we come into contact with?

Acts 3

S—The S stands for **Scripture**

O—The O stands for **Observation**

A—The A stands for **Application**

K—The K stands for **Kneeling in Prayer**

There is salvation in no one else,

for there is no other name

under heaven given among men

by which we must be saved.

Acts 4:12

Reflection Question:

Peter and John remained firm in their faith, despite knowing what happened to Jesus when He spoke against the scribes.

Do you allow fear to consume your choices to speak out about God or do you allow faith to continue to show through?

Acts 4

S—The S stands for *Scripture*

O—The O stands for *Observation*

A—The A stands for *Application*

K—The K stands for *Kneeling in Prayer*

We must obey God rather than men.

Acts 5:29

Reflection Question:

Peter and the Apostles were ordered to not teach about Jesus. They refused claiming that they would follow God's instructions.

Name a time when you have been asked to not speak about God. How did you respond?

Acts 5

S—The S stands for *Scripture*

O—The O stands for *Observation*

A—The A stands for *Application*

K—The K stands for *Kneeling in Prayer*

The word of God continued to increase, and the number of the disciples multiplied greatly.

Acts 6:7

Reflection Question:

The Apostles knew they had limits. They could not be effective in all the areas that needed to be filled in the ministry.

Are there areas in your life that you need to delegate or step away from so you can be effective in the areas God is calling you to lead?

Acts 6

S—The S stands for ***Scripture***

O—The O stands for ***Observation***

A—The A stands for ***Application***

K—The K stands for ***Kneeling in Prayer***

He (Stephen), full of the Holy Spirit,

gazed into heaven and saw the glory of God,

and Jesus standing at the right hand of God.

Acts 7:55

Reflection Question:

Stephen was persecuted for his beliefs. Yet he stood firm, even though he was to face death.

How has your walk with God caused you to be persecuted?

Acts 7

S—The S stands for *Scripture*

O—The O stands for *Observation*

A—The A stands for *Application*

K—The K stands for *Kneeling in Prayer*

Those who were scattered

went about preaching the word.

Acts 8:4

Reflection Question:

God put Philip in the position to minister to the Eunuch.

Name a time when God has caused your paths to cross with someone who needed you to minister to them.

Acts 8

S—The S stands for *Scripture*

O—The O stands for *Observation*

A—The A stands for *Application*

K—The K stands for *Kneeling in Prayer*

And He (Saul) said,

"Who are you, Lord?"

And he said, "I am Jesus,

whom you are persecuting."

Acts 9:5

Reflection Question:

Saul is a great reminder that God can use our past as a great testimony to reach others.

In what ways has God used your testimony to reach and touch others?

Acts 9

S—The S stands for *Scripture*

O—The O stands for *Observation*

A—The A stands for *Application*

K—The K stands for *Kneeling in Prayer*

God shows no partiality, but in every nation anyone who fears him and does what is right is acceptable to him.

Acts 10:34,35

Reflection Question:

Peter had been focusing on the Jewish community. Yet God laid it on Peter's heart that salvation was for all people.

Name a time when you wrestled with the fact that someone was possibly undeserving of God's gift of salvation. How did you overcome it?

Acts 10

S—The S stands for *Scripture*

O—The O stands for *Observation*

A—The A stands for *Application*

K—The K stands for *Kneeling in Prayer*

In Antioch the disciples

were first called Christians.

Acts 11:26

Reflection Question:

Peter was questioned about reaching out to the Gentile community.

Have you ever been questioned about reaching out to someone who God has laid on your heart? How did you respond?

S—The S stands for *Scripture*

O—The O stands for *Observation*

A—The A stands for *Application*

K—The K stands for *Kneeling in Prayer*

But the word of God

increased and multiplied.

Acts 12:24

Reflection Question:

Peter was rescued by God from the hands of Herod.

Have you ever had a time when God has stepped in and delivered you from a situation?

Acts 12

S—The S stands for *Scripture*

O—The O stands for *Observation*

A—The A stands for *Application*

K—The K stands for *Kneeling in Prayer*

He raised up David to be their king,

of whom he testified and said,

'I have found in David the son of Jesse

a man after my heart, who will do all my will.'

Acts 13:22

Reflection Question:

Paul and Barnabas spoke a message that was not received well.

Have you ever had a conviction laid on your heart that was not received well? How did you handle it?

Acts 13

S—The S stands for *Scripture*

O—The O stands for *Observation*

A—The A stands for *Application*

K—The K stands for *Kneeling in Prayer*

Through many tribulations

we must enter the kingdom of God.

Acts 14:22

Reflection Question:

Paul and Barnabas were referred to as gods. Yet, they remained humble and pointed all praise back to God.

How do you remain humble when you are praised?

Acts 14

S—The S stands for *Scripture*

O—The O stands for *Observation*

A—The A stands for *Application*

K—The K stands for *Kneeling in Prayer*

We believe that we will be saved

through the grace of the Lord Jesus.

Acts 15:11

Reflection Question:

Throughout history Christians have struggled with unity and contention.

How have you handled these issues throughout your life?

Acts 15

S—The S stands for *Scripture*

O—The O stands for *Observation*

A—The A stands for *Application*

K—The K stands for *Kneeling in Prayer*

Believe in the Lord Jesus,

and you will be saved,

you and your household.

Acts 16:31

Reflection Question:

Obeying the call of the Lord in our lives often brings about unexpected trials, but blessing for our obedience is certain to come.

What blessings has God given you when you followed a call He's given you?

Acts 16

S—The S stands for *Scripture*

O—The O stands for *Observation*

A—The A stands for *Application*

K—The K stands for *Kneeling in Prayer*

In him we live and move

and have our being.

Acts 17:28

Reflection Question:

Paul was unafraid of preaching the gospel of Christ. He did not fear what man could do to him.

How can you be more like Paul and share the gospel with others?

S—The S stands for *Scripture*

O—The O stands for *Observation*

A—The A stands for *Application*

K—The K stands for *Kneeling in Prayer*

Do not be afraid,

but go on speaking

and do not be silent.

Acts 18:9

Reflection Question:

Not only did Paul preach the gospel of Jesus Christ, but he spent significant amounts of time teaching and encouraging fellow believers.

What can you do to teach and/or encourage a fellow believer today?

Acts 18

S—The S stands for *Scripture*

O—The O stands for *Observation*

A—The A stands for *Application*

K—The K stands for *Kneeling in Prayer*

The word of the Lord

continued to increase

and prevail mightily.

Acts 19:20

Reflection Question:

Demetrius' business was at stake because of Paul's preaching the truth of Jesus Christ at Ephesus.

Have you ever been faced with difficulty or loss of a job because of your faith?

Acts 19

S—The S stands for **Scripture**

O—The O stands for **Observation**

A—The A stands for **Application**

K—The K stands for **Kneeling in Prayer**

It is more blessed to give than to receive.

Acts 20:35

Reflection Question:

Paul knew he wouldn't see the believers at Ephesus again. He prepared and encouraged them for the difficulties that would come their way in the future. He was not concerned with himself in any way.

How can you be more mission focused in your life, ultimately following both Jesus' and Paul's example?

Acts 20

S—The S stands for *Scripture*

O—The O stands for *Observation*

A—The A stands for *Application*

K—The K stands for *Kneeling in Prayer*

Then Paul answered,

"What are you doing, weeping and breaking my heart?

For I am ready not only to be imprisoned but even to die

in Jerusalem for the name of the Lord Jesus."

Acts 21:13

Reflection Question:

Paul's heart and life were solely devoted to Christ. He did not fear a martyr's death.

If faced with this being part of your future, how do you think you would respond?

S—The S stands for *Scripture*

O—The O stands for *Observation*

A—The A stands for *Application*

K—The K stands for *Kneeling in Prayer*

And now why do you wait? Rise and be baptized and wash away your sins, calling on his name.

Acts 22:16

Reflection Question:

Paul was not hesitant to give his testimony, even though his past was laden with sin. His life proves that God CAN and WILL use ANYONE who has a willing heart.

Who can you share your testimony with today? How has God used you in spite of your past?

Acts 22

S—The S stands for *Scripture*

O—The O stands for *Observation*

A—The A stands for *Application*

K—The K stands for *Kneeling in Prayer*

The following night the Lord stood by him and said,

"Take courage, for as you have testified

to the facts about me in Jerusalem,

so you must testify also in Rome."

Acts 23:11

Reflection Question:

God revealed that He was not yet finished with Paul and that he would give his testimony in Rome.

When have you thought that God was finished with you, but He used you again?

Acts 23

S—The S stands for *Scripture*

O—The O stands for *Observation*

A—The A stands for *Application*

K—The K stands for *Kneeling in Prayer*

I always take pains

to have a clear conscience

toward both God and man.

Acts 24:16

Reflection Question:

Felix heard Paul's case and found no reason to make a ruling, he even hoped that Paul would pay him off to be released. Instead he kept him bound just to satisfy the Jews.

Have you been faced with unjust judgment in your life? If so, how did you respond?

Acts 24

S—The S stands for *Scripture*

O—The O stands for *Observation*

A—The A stands for *Application*

K—The K stands for *Kneeling in Prayer*

I do not seek to escape death.

Acts 25:11

Reflection Question:

Nothing brought against Paul could be proven, yet no ruler would let him go.

How have you responded to untrue accusations that couldn't be proven in your life?

Acts 25

S—The S stands for *Scripture*

O—The O stands for *Observation*

A—The A stands for *Application*

K—The K stands for *Kneeling in Prayer*

To open their eyes, so that they may turn from darkness to light and from the power of Satan to God, that they may receive forgiveness of sins and a place among those who are sanctified by faith in me.

Acts 26:18

Reflection Question:

Though Paul was imprisoned, he was allowed to speak for himself and give his testimony again, just as God promised.

Has God ever given you another opportunity to share your testimony with someone? If so, did you take advantage of the opportunity?

Acts 26

S—The S stands for *Scripture*

O—The O stands for *Observation*

A—The A stands for *Application*

K—The K stands for *Kneeling in Prayer*

So take heart, men, for I have faith in God

that it will be exactly as I have been told.

Acts 27:25

Reflection Question:

Paul was able to witness again for Christ and reveal what God had promised, that all the lives aboard the ship would be saved.

How have you been able to share God's promises with others?

Acts 27

S—The S stands for **Scripture**

O—The O stands for **Observation**

A—The A stands for **Application**

K—The K stands for **Kneeling in Prayer**

Let it be known to you that this salvation of God

has been sent to the Gentiles; they will listen.

Acts 28:28

Reflection Question:

No matter where Paul went or was taken, he shared his testimony and allowed God to work through him.

Are you living a surrendered life? How can you allow God to work through you today?

Acts 28

S—The S stands for *Scripture*

O—The O stands for *Observation*

A—The A stands for *Application*

K—The K stands for *Kneeling in Prayer*

44220966R00037

Made in the USA
Lexington, KY
25 August 2015